AMERI(C)A

Eddy Duhan

Books by Eddy Duhan

ALL MEN ARE LIKE FLIES:
and other long lost poemsongs

PRAYERS OF THE ANCIENTS

STAND UP MICHAEL:
Long Lake Anthology of Poets

WORD PICTURES:
The Showtime Journals (rewriting music scores)

AMERI(C)A
classified

www.amazon.com/Eddy-Duhan/e/B00JAEUGPQ

*Thanks to Chris Justice for the cover painting
of the American flag, and to Charles Bukowski
for the influence and inspiration.
Jan Duhan for Photoshop
"Legacy" and "Disciples of Honor"
written by Eddy Duhan
and Dr. Arnold Nerenberg,
special thanks to
John Andrew Schreiner
for the prayers and friendship*

longlakemusic@yahoo.com

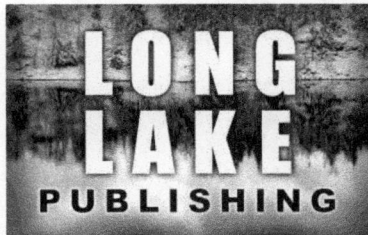

LONG LAKE PUBLISHING

This book is dedicated to Jesus,
President Donald Trump and his family,
WikiLeaks, and Veritas,
and to Sarah and Hailey for the
prodding, goading, agitation,
and good humor!

Eddy,

They said we could never do it.

But last night you showed the world that America will once again be a country of, for, and by the PEOPLE.

You fought like a winner, you defied all odds, and history will forever remember the role you played in taking our country back.

I never could've done it without you, Eddy. Your contributions, your sacrifices, and your unyielding commitment to our movement made last night possible!

Last night we learned that America is still a beacon of hope where the impossible is possible.

For far too long, we've heard Washington politicians give the excuse that "it can't be done." They say we can't balance the budget, we can't stop corruption, we can't control the border, we can't bring jobs back to our country.

I REFUSE to accept that it can't be done. This is the country that declared its independence, won two world wars, and landed a man on the moon. This is America. We can and we WILL get it done.

Now it's time to start uniting our country and binding the wounds of our divided nation. I promise to be a president for ALL Americans. I will work for you. I will fight for you. And I will win for you.

You will soon remember what it's like to win as an American.

Thank you and God bless you,

Donald J. Trump

TRUMP
PENCE
MAKE AMERICA GREAT AGAIN!
2016

TRUMP BOARD OF DIRECTORS

Membership Certificate

In gratitude for all your generous support of Donald Trump's 2016 presidential campaign as a member of the Trump Board of Directors, and in recognition of your allegiance to our strong America First agenda, this certificate is hereby presented to:

Eddy Duhan

Thank you for your financial help, your patriotism, and your active involvement in our movement. Citizens like you are the reason why we will Make America Great Again.

Donald J. Trump

table of *(c)*ontents

the dark red (c)loud of purgatory…

merry (C)hristmas and a happy new year…

mine eyes have seen the glory
of the (c)oming of the Lord...

1.
the (C) stands for ...

1. let's make America great again

I was born in 1954
'On the Waterfront' won the award
Grace Kelly for 'Country Girl'
over Judy Garland's 'A Star is Born'

let's make America great again
and remember how it was way back then…

my dad drove a Hudson Hornet
the monster of the stock car crash
it was last year they made it
before they had to merge with Nash

'Little Things Mean A lot'
was number one on the chart
and the rat pack was hot
Sinatra sang 'Young at Heart'

we all had a date with Elvis
with a 'Blue Moon ln Kentucky'
'I Don't Care If The Sun Don't Shine'
'There's Good Rockin' Tonight'

'From Here to Eternity'
won Oscar in that year
and Eisenhower met with aliens
when he disappeared

8/25/15

2. **the whistleblower**

there's a fly on the wall
God's ears and eyes in every place
like Elisha who knew the secrets
from the kings own private space

the bravery of exposing darkness
like Snowden, WikiLeaks, & Veritas
have done this world such a kindness
to give their freedom for the cause

.

God help the whistleblower
who helps to keep us free
Godspeed them from the danger
the hound of heaven at their feet

help me to see the angels
who are circled all around me
strike the enemy with blindness
and give your servant eyes to see

don't let sicko's hurt the children
tie a stone around their neck
sink them in the deepest ocean
give them what they don't expect

11/21/16

3. **maybe I will win**

maybe I will win the lottery
maybe I'll go crazy
maybe Donald Trump will call me
or maybe my lawyer or
a rich lesbian from Newport Coast
maybe I'll be reincarnated as a catfish
or find a sack of money
floating down the river

I need help
I am an old man being eaten
by television and
you

spin spin spin
light a candle
My bones ache my soul aches
I wake every hour or two
think of how the teacher
used the nasty seaword
in front of the grade 9 class
to explain double standards
while reading Of Mice and Men;

"the man is called a player when he is unfaithful,
 but the woman is a (c)..t!"

keeping up with the Kardashians
burning my blood like Champaign
cocaine and gasoline
making the supervisor grin
my words are only dropping's
and scratching's
on the bottom of a
birdcage mirror

10/8/16

4. **raccoon eyes**

I like D.J. Trump
he can get so indignant
he can snap rip and burn
with wonderful energetic words
he can lay it down off the cuff
bright and writhing
create a stink of blood and murder
and then there is the tenderness
that you see when he is with his
beautiful European wife
I like D.J. Trump
he can talk about Jesus Christ
like he lives right next door
and he can describe Muslim terrorists
so well that you hate them
I like D.J. Trump
but I'm glad I haven't met him
or sat across from him in a cafe
while he looks at you
with his steely reverse
raccoon eyes.

10/8/16

5. **fiction**

leaving the bookstore with my daughter.
she is carrying 2 new books to read, and I picked up a
Bukowski, and the Cure's greatest hits from the bargain hasbin.
then to the beach to listen to music and read...
"21 pilots aren't bad...but you have got to hear some really good
old school!" I say, as I push in the cd. Robert Smith begins his
incredible emotional vocal outbursts!

my little girl is a big fan of 21 Pilots and she tells me, "One of
the guys in the band is a Christian, dad!"

"oh yeah? how do you know that?"

"he has a tattoo of a cross on his arm!"

"Ok cool...how did they come up with that name? is it because
they are saying 'we're old enough to drink and drive?' I joke.

"huh?" it flies over her head. "I think it comes from a made up
story about an airplane mechanic who made a decision between
installing faulty parts and feeding his family. one of the planes
he worked on ended up crashing. there were 21 pilots on it. I
guess they want to promote the idea of making right choices..."
she explains to me.

"wow! so it is a memorial for the 21 dead pilots?"

"no dad, the story is FICTION!"

"Hey, the Cure was on Fiction Records. What a coincidence!" I
say as Robert sings, 'I will always love you...'

10/9/16

6. don't kid yourself

don't kid yourself
he defied all the odds-
I'm told Trump can't
become president now
he's being sued
by a girl
she has hired Gloria Allred
oh my oh my

well something will stop
everybody dead in their tracks
sooner or later
brain damage, wikileaks, sex tapes,
drugs, rock and roll, roll of dice

when Jesus Christ came
I'm sure he knew his
would be the cross
and you know how that
turned out
no matter how they try
they can't nail him
down to one...

so they keep looking
for a more effective one
but
he keeps resurrecting

in the meantime, we all know
what it's about, we dismiss it,
we forget it,
we move on
take a shot of vinegar
from a whiskey glass
and keep kidding yourself   *10/12/16*

7. **speck of light**

so what is this body but a
fallen angel
caught inside
staring into a mirror
reconciling the passing of time
or the reflection of wallflowers
from behind
arms move head turns eyes bright
seeing a glimpse
of Christ in the darkness
through one small
speck of light

10/12/16

8. amnesty and amnesia

have you ever lived somewhere
where you can't sleep
car horns, helicopters,
fireworks exploding
I lie awake thinking about
songs like fiery arrows,
youtube, elections, poetry
I think about John Fahey's bones
laying in his grave
where he has no need of open (C) tuning

I think of Chelsea Clinton Hubbell
and Danney Williams Clinton,
and wonder if they will ever
get to connect with their real fathers
and come to an understanding

and your arm gets caught
under your body
and it goes numb
it is the only part of you
that has fallen asleep
but soon everything will be awakening

so now you arise
before the sun
and not remember anything
whether reality or imagining
with amnesty and amnesia
to the smell of the
automatic coffee machine brewing

10/13/16

9. **Hillary**

wikiwiki definition:
burning paint
wrinkling on a wall,
an old used tire
stripped and flat,
a house sinking
in the sand,
a hoarders bathtub
full of trash,
a barking dog
behind a fence,
a radio that
you can't turn off,
with A Check To A Queen
Count Dracula's Great Love
and The Queens Of Evil,
see BDSM: actress Haydée Politoff,

10/14/16

23

10. thank God for wikileaks

yes on Donald Trump
no on Hillary Clinton
yes on citizens united
no on death penalty repeal
yes on condoms for sex films
no on overblown school spending
yes on shortened death penalty appeals
no on pot reefer blunt legalizing
yes on English proficiency
no on the tax extension
yes on 2/3 voter approval for tax raising
no on gun background checks
yes on keeping single use plastic bags
no on fees for plastic bags
yes on Kamala Harris maybe not
no on Loretta Sanchez
someone told me
that the reason
Loretta Sanchez
missed so many votes in Congress
was because she was busy working
on a top secret project
for the government
(to make the FEMA Camps
operational)

soon they will be herding us up
into FEMA Camps for our votes
and they will crop dust us
like desert locusts
to keep us down-
they will have no anchor store's there
and no aluminum siding...
ohhh, they will start slowly,
maybe housing Syrian refugees at first, then
BAMSKOCKALOCK

"conspiracy theorist!" you say.
well, some form of the word
conspiracy
is used 10 times in the bible.

thank God for WikiLeaks.

10/16/16

11. the first and second coming

when Moses first went
up into Mount Sinai
he had a prophetic
encounter with God
in a burning tree
a clear picture
of Jesus on the cross
a prophecy of
deliverance
of Christ's first advent
holy ground

on his second coming
to Mount Sinai
he came down with the law
to judge
a clear prophecy of
Christ's second coming
to judge the world
before they stepped into
eternity

the mockers said,
"where did he go
where is the promise of his coming
he died up there in the clouds
of the mountain
let's make our own way
because he is not returning!"

and what did he find
when he did come down…
a dark apocalyptic scene?
NO-but a party, a big peace fest, dancing
around the golden abomination

which is Lucifer, himself,
who comes first
pretending to be Jesus, and he
will destroy many through
peace.

the line was drawn
the ground split open
and swallowed up the
New World Order

10/16/16

12. **look at her**

look at her
a withered woman
yeah, she has
been through
a lot
now she is kept under cover
and the house shakes
rattles and rolls
she tries to smile
but can't get it out
they say a piece of the roof
broke free and fell on her head
they say she was tough
and could weather
anything, yet...
the light peeks through the hole
but they won't let anyone in to see
the spin doctors have looked
for the pipes
and wires
but there is nothing left
they were torn out
years ago

so let's make her
president

10/16/16

13 . **more poems**

my daughter walks in
and says, "Hailey and I want you
to write more poems
about humpity dumpityTrumpity"

"really?" I ask, "why?"

"because, we like it!"

"how about if I write poems
about Hillary instead?"

"ok, she said, "then Hillary too..."

so here I am
writing useless poems
like a dorky little schoolboy
for silly high school girls
surely, I must be crazy
so here it goes,
but first I must forgive myself
for what they want me to compose

there is no greater man
there is no better woman
for this cat and dog fight
between Hitlery and wandering Jew
he scrambles with pitchfork
he breaks every egg
she scratches and snarls
and stirs a poisonous brew

like all bloodsport fighters
Sugar Ray and Babe
the odds are in Vegas
against poor us they say

the whole world is red hot
with a thunderous groan
as they lean in to see
just who drives it home.

10/21/16

14. **the horserace**

Donald is a closer
that's where he really shines
the Glengarry Glenn Ross
he comes up from behind
a 16-to-one long shot
and easily sets the pace
ran like he was mad as hell
and quickly closed the space

now it's on the home stretch
now it's down to two
a nose to nose with Crooked C
and Tacky Horsey Glue
Crooked is on steroids
the cameraman a sniper
the racing forms are slanted
one sided in her favor

Donald runs with head down
he pulls ahead again
Hillary seems satisfied
that the fix is in
the payout is the future
the odds are on the crime
the audience is thunder
the announcer is stone blind

10/23/16

15. **drain the swamp**

the crocodiles of midnight
tearing at the bones
the hippos of early morning
go slowly wading home

all the greatest words
of all the greatest men
are not so great after all
when they meet their end

grief tailed Sunday-eyed
under sheets of rain
the rotting smell of dying flesh
overflowing with disdain

drain the swamp
cover it over
with a new way a new time
and a new kind of alligator

16. **the (c) stands for…**

Clinton
        crooked
                criminal
                      clueless
                            cash
                                  cryptic
                                        commie
crocodile
        crazy
            crook
                concussion
                        cheat
                            corrupt
                                conniving

(c)leptomaniac
                Chelsea
                    coarse
                      con
                        calculating
                              condescending

but not_
        confidential,
        and surely not
        classified!
                YOU EVEN STOLE KLEPTOMANIAIC
        BY SPELLING IT WITH A (C)!

maybe it stands for Comey,

or "Christ's Cross".

17. **May 23, 2002**

magic magnificent Thursday
the birthday of my little girl
a significant day after all
for such off events of this world

it was the same day in Iceland
the 55 parties clause is signed
of the Kyoto protocol
after it was ratified

Pope John Paul was in Bulgaria
George Bush was in Berlin
Sam Snead the golfer died
'Foolish' by Ashanti was number one

a king of France a Chinese Emperor
a birthday shared in history
with some notable artists and composers
and the father of taxonomy

she's like a flower in the ruins
for this old battle-weary man
springs up love like it was meant to be
and quickens like the morning sun

11/25/16

18. Paisley

Paisley why don't you come home
Paisley why don't you come home
you been gone so long
since the day you was born

well your momma said it's time to roll
well your momma said it's time to go
but you cry so loud
and let everybody know

like Bessie Smith ole' Le Chat Noir
Bessie Smith that ole' Le Chat Noir
you lived under a box
at the back of the park

the little girls come to take you home
the little girls come to take you in
they don't know who you are
or where you've been.

you jumped on down from the window pane
jumped on down from the window pane
take a look around
and jumped back up again

Paisley why don't you come home
Paisley why don't you come home
you been gone so long
my how you have grown

5/23/16

19. please Mr. next President!

please Mr. next President
shake out that welfare line
got no money in my pocket
can't be paying all the time
for those chasing dreams
on the government dime

please Mr. next President
put missiles in Ukraine
tell that jackboot Putin
he ain't gonna be
no Stalin or Hitler
no Stalin or Hitler again

gotta repeal them blues
untie those knots
follow the rules
enforce the laws

please Mr. next President
get back our national pride
bow down to China and India
show'em our backside
like old glory let it shine
like old glory let it shine

2/28/14

2.
your past (c)omes back waving a white flag…

20. your past comes back waving a white flag

I was living in the shadows
like an overstaying guest
like Bukowski in a rooming house
like Hemmingway in Paris

hiding out in plain sight
living with the Christians
working with the aliens
and running with the lions

I have lived inside a '68 white and yellow Cadillac
in a green econoline Frod van
on a ship in LA harbor
and with members of the Donna Summers Band

I have been
a landscaper
a gardener
a bricklayer
a salesman
a student
a poet
a lineman
a homeless drifter
a telephone operator
a songwriter
a janitor
a recording engineer
one thing or another

I had a few girlfriends back in those days,
there was Nancy
from Salt Lake City
her dad was a scientist
and a doctor

he invented
artificial arteries
he said to me once:

"it's hard to get funding, artificial arteries aren't that sexy!
now my colleague, Jervis who worked on the artificial heart
valve machine, that was a sexy funding machine!" he while
clutching his young new Japanese wife.
Nancy fumed beside me, because he had abandoned her mother
and her for someone else so young and beautiful.

"she used to be my friend, I introduced her to my dad! she is the
same age as me. NOW MY MOTHER HAS NOTHING!"

I guess some people want artificial everything…

we never saw or talked to each other again after that.
I guess she just wanted to drag the trash out
in front of her dad to hurt him like he hurt her.
'see DAD, I can hit back with this going nowhere, uneducated
loser of a door to door salesman, and
a hasbin poet musician that's never bin!"

_then there was Deb who wanted
to marry a Christian
rock star
she finally did but it was not me.
she ended it by saying,
"you seem so naive
I hope coming here doesn't change you
I hope you never lose that innocence."

I
   l o s t

       it
          on
             the
                  downward
                        spiral.

(then Ronald Reagan granted me amnesty…
and it was all uphill after that.)

then there is always the girl that you loved,
but never loved you back…

your past comes back to haunt you
most of the time it comes crawling. taunting, hissing ,
and sticking its tongue out like a blue flame
but on rare occasions it comes
waving a white flag
with a friendly smile

"I tried to contact you for years" she wrote.
"I feel so bad about the way I treated you.
I was sure you never wanted to talk to me again, or ever have
anything to do with me.
you were always so nice and giving, and I wasn't very nice to
you back then. I want to say I'm sorry…
IamnowasuccessfulartistinNewYorkIfinallygotmarriedatage50an
damveryhappywithmylife!

so tell me about your life…
I love that you have a young daughter…makes my heart smile
whenever I think of her."

yes, and you realize things worked out for the best,
that your lives went in vastly different directions…

but today the IMOJI button heart looks redder

and the sun shines brighter like the yellow
smiley happy face

and for once the grass looks greener
from where I'm standing
for both me, and her…
but there's no IMOJ I to describe
how to show you how you feel

then she wrote, "please don't tell me that you are voting
for Donald Trump! that would make me howl!"

"well, it doesn't matter who I vote for in California
because Hillary has the electoral votes sown up here,
and the action will be in the swing States…"
I responded in the most diplomatic way I could

I haven't heard from her since……..oh, wait!

21. exercise in futility

when I get the inclination
to play the lottery
first go to the Walmart
and find a new
lock with a combination
in the hardware department
and if I can't guess
the combo
in eight or nine tries or less
then I will forego the lottery

prayer doesn't help
God knows
the big win at his expense
will do more harm than good
that's just how it goes
so he will never answer that
selfish plea
it is an exercise in futility
if you win 20 million
you're on your own, without me

it's like Steinbeck's Pearl
and the curse of Aladdin
I would say be careful then
with what you wish for again, and again
and ask yourself
has this ever happened before
a dog that catches itself by the tale
a fish that becomes a nightmare whale
when you can't awaken anymore
as the forces of nature devour
and the best that you can hope for
is die in your sleep forevermore

10/26/16

22. **wasting words**

not willing to die
but ready to kill

drink the cool-aid
take the pill

as the shark swims
thorough the veins

looks for the heart
but nothing remains

wasting words
at a stunning pace

the melting earth
the human race

if you can't stand the heat
get out of the kitchen

but I'm not in the kitchen
I'm here in the oven

who said that?
was it Harry Truman

or was it a song
by Randy Newman?

23. the riddle

imagine Hillary
in a jail cell with no door
a jail cell with no window
only a table and a mirror

she can get out it's possible
if she can just solve the riddle
she has the crooked outlook
where nothing is inescapable

she looks into the mirror
sees two halves of the table
and says "two halves make a hole"
then crawls right through the middle

10/29/16

45

24. Donald the pageantist

ok, here it is
my 14 year old daughter
asked me, "aren't you going to
write anything about Donald
Trump the sexual predator?"

so this is the truth as I see it...
I will admit that Donald the Pageantist has been
a horn-dog.
he is powerful man that
obviously loves beautiful women, after all he owns the Miss
Universe Pageant.
not to mention he was married 3 times
and is now married to a beautiful young
European model.

I chalk DJT up to male testosterone, and personal failures
usually, it tapers out with age responsibility and repose

the progressives are worse
they feign outrage
Michael Robinson
says he was "shaken to the core"
over Trump's words...really?
I think it was Joan River's words
that really shook him to the core.
it is common internet knowledge
that Michelle is a transvestite,
and the kids were adopted from Morocco,
not to mention that Hillary is a bisexual
who cucked Janet Reno, Huma Abedin,
and had Chelsea with Webster Hubbell,

then there are the real sexual predators
like Bill Clinton, and Anthony Weiner,

the Twitter spitter…all hypocrites!
we all know the faces and the stories…

it is like the pot calling the kettle Danney Williams!
the Democratic Party, the party of Andrew Jackson,
of broken Indian treaties and reservations,
of slavery and the Klu Klux Klan,
of voting against suffrage…
the party of gays, gay marriage, transvestites,
sexual perversion, hard core predators,
pornography and abortions
media blackouts and cover-ups

this is a bloodsport
CUT, SLASH, STAB!
anything to "win this motherf**ker!"
because it is all about control
and power over others
sexual,
political
financial
it doesn't matter what the weapon
use anything to bring your opponent down

but God chose
David the Psalmist
to be leader over his people
(like He may be choosing Donald the Pageantist)
and David like Donald was a horn-dog too
ask his 8 wives, Mikal, Achino'am, Abigail, Ma'akah, Abital,
Chaggith, Abital, Eg lal, and Bathsheba
his water, his love, his royalty, his pet,
his festal, his dew, his heifer, and his oath

and he tapered off
on the young beauty Abishag

whose name means to error
or to make a mistake…

25. the diabolical narcissist's prayer

that didn't happen.
and if it did happen, it wasn't that bad.
and if it was that bad, that's not a big deal.
and if it is a big deal, that's not my fault.
and if it was my fault, I didn't mean it.
and if I did mean it...
you deserved it.
amen.

(unknown)

26. **kayfabe**

just one more week to go
then we all should know
according to Joan of Arc
the fix was in long ago
maybe so maybe so

she says he doesn't want the job
but he was her only hope
to steal these former United States
when she's got us on the ropes
maybe so maybe so

he wins only if he loses
he gets to enhance his brand
Cloward-Piven was set in motion
it was always baked into the plan
maybe so maybe so

kayfabe with the crooked tag team
blind sycophancy runs its course
leopards never change their spots
and the rhetoric is all a farce
maybe so maybe so

I say let's just let him win
make him finish what he began
he's far better for entertainment
than a cackling witch for president
maybe so maybe so

11/1/16

27. sex slave island

they all ride the Lolita Express
fly with Epstein to his Island of Sex
the Saudis give them children to rape
Huma Weiner Hillary Bill and all the rest

the FBI and the NYPD have the evidence
plus so much more on Wieners computer
it shows espionage with the Muslim Brotherhood
and top secret emails sold to the lowest bidder

lock her up
Hillary for prison
burn out the snake pit
of their elite globalism

there are Democrats and Republicans
slithering in the dark cabal
BHO and Mikey are probably in on the scam
the media and government know about it all

11/3/16

28. this is nothing

she's got
the server
the Foundation
the Lolita Express
Hillary's America
Global Initiative
WikiLeaks
Clinton Cash
Veritas
the FBI
Weiner's computer
the NYPD
Whitewater
Travel Gate
Billy the rapist
and Benghazi
Loretta Lynch
Debbie Wasserman
Donna Brazile
and a rigged primary

bleach it scrub it wipe it clean...
"you mean with a cloth or something?"
to quote a line from Wag the Dog,
"this is nothing! this is NOTHING!"

11/3/16

29. **spirit cooking**

what's on the menu
at Sex Slave Island
the black art of spirit cooking
raping kidnapped children

hotdog is a little boy
pizza is a little girl
handkerchief is a condom
map is code for sperm trail

mixed with mother's milk
fresh blood and fresh semen
drink on earthquake nights
a witches brew a black art coven

with a sharp knife cut deeply
into the middle finger
of your left hand
eat the pain
and wickedness of Aleister Crowley

11/4/16

30. Podesta the primary poet with a megaphone

Bernie needs to be ground to a pulp
where would you stick the knife in?
we can't start believing our own bullshit
crush him as hard as you can

Hillary is going to blow it
she is repeating her past mistakes
she is getting milked by her consultants
while giving paid speeches to banks

if there is one thing in this world
that could bring her down
it is the cycling money wheel
that's going around and around

foreign donations and paid speeches
red alerts ringing bells and warning signs
it will all be megaphoned everywhere
about her hustling for gold in the mines

let's have her come out against Keystone
tell voters what they want to hear
to help distract from the emails
give her a legitimate way to steer clear

11/6/16

31. blackberry

blackberry singing in the dead of night
take this song that all the spies can hear
all your words
be very careful about the danger in the air

blackberry singing in the dead of night
take this hammer and make them disappear
all your words
whatever made you think that they could be secure

blackberry die
blackberry die
into the heart of the dark black night

11/6/16

32. ode to James Comey

Jim Comey is deep in the tank
he was on the board of a drug cartel bank
before he led the FBI
he plays both sides as good guy bad guy

"I get a big fat I told you so
on Comey being a bad choice"
says Podesta in his emails...
Obama must have kicked his ass

to go through 650,000 emails
in only over just one week
he must think we all are stupid
to say "there's nothing here to see"

Comey says, "Blah blah blah.."
So keep your eyes on WikiLeaks
don't waste time when it's on the line
on cheaters playing dirty pool for keeps

so boys and girls
of the file and rank
keep on throwing them
tarnished badges in his tank

11/6/16

33. **the village queen**

the masquerade parade.
resembling what might appear
a marching band death chant
in a future year
the village queen's retinue
fast approaching near.
military waltzing,
and drums striking fear.

same old tragedy,
on a different face
same old confusion,
said in a different way.
same old harlot,
riding on the back
same old breakdown,
Shakespearean play.

standing on the gallows,
are three unfortunate men
Plato and the future Pope,
and the poet Leonard Cohen.
Plato's mouth is taped shut,
the future Pope speaks first:
"this blood and wine you drink,
will never quench your thirst."

she looks at Leonard Cohen,
he says to her so warm
"you stand there in your blizzard
and I can feel your storm."

she nods
and pulls the lever
and they swing
back and forth.

"time and tide will answer all
for what it's worth to hang your hope
on extreme psychotic and high maintenance!"
says Plato, when he breaks the rope.

34. the ways of nature

doesn't want perfection
it goes against the nature
would rather be involved with
polishing the armor

love is kind of strange
it's hard to understand
like the ways of nature
a woman with a man

a diamond in rough
a serpent on a rock
hard truths will unwind
deep mysteries will unlock

like a bird in the air
like a ship on the sea
held and suspended there
tossed and floating gracefully

35. the queen of heaven

I read Revelation on Patmos,
with a rooster crowing in the distance.

took Saint Paul's Journey to Mars Hill,
saw Corinth through the construction fence.

Mary icons with instead of Christ,
like Athena holding out the snake.

big mama and the satellite,
the queen of heaven dropped the cake.

36. fly raven fly

there's a raven tearing up,
from the bottom of a tree.
then flies beyond the weathervane,
of a whale in the sea.

heading for Elijah
who is waiting by the stream.
past the hissing sprinklers,
and the reservoir of extremes.

over the casino in the holy land,
over the whorehouse in Tel Aviv,
the pagan temple on a mountain,
and the gaudy shrine at Calvary.

fly raven fly,
and tell him what you see.

37. **the prize**

something that you dreamed of
to show the prize in your hand
walk in radiating pleasure
you can hardly stand
you want to share the moment
but your told to be seated
been to see to the doctor
you must tell who's been cheated

why is it that the worst blows
come at the highest peaks
like a knife through a sacrifice
this one plays for keeps

the disease is the lie
not to love in any way
intent for your response
yet there's nothing you can say
but to sit there all dumbfounded
holding innocence in your hands
now the prize is bleeding out
what forgiveness understands

38. **better not to know**

there's a man
a ghost in the wind
wandering alone
like a chameleon
the mark of Cain
it doesn't show
if you can see it
just let him go

sometimes it's better not to know
sometimes it's better not to know
whispers a voice from way down low
sometimes it's better not to know

in the shadows
in the rain
in the silhouette
of a moving train
you can see him
passing slow
from a garden
into a ghetto

39. the flame

he shall run the world over
through China, USA, EC, and Israel...

but first to the Greek Islands
where the flame once burning died

the flame of the Seven Churches
the flame of Olympic glory

the flame quenched in the ruins
of a third world empire's story

from Babylon to the Medes and Persians
and the Roman New World Order

to globalism's deadly wound
inflicted mortal then was healed

to the flame that burns eternal
when the truth will be been revealed

40. practice makes perfect

practice makes perfect
when is time to do your lessons
and you really really
really want to know
practice makes perfect
just try a little bit harder
and you learn
how to make things go

if Alexander Graham Bell
stopped right at the tel-
-aphone would never be invented
and you could not call home
if Orville and Wilbur Wright
never made that very first flight
we would still be on the ground
not landing on the moon

when the teacher says the alphabet
remember it and don't forget
it's a building block the very next step
to where you want to get
Audrey can play concert violin
Sarah can be the President
Henry can be a rocket man
if they never quit

cause practice makes perfect
practice makes perfect sense

41. born from above

she picks at her fingers
trying to peel out of her skin
you can tell by the anguish
she's never felt comfortable in

did you know we are linked
to that time the angels fell?
then poured into these flesh bodies
like water to be drawn from a well

the widow and the clay pots of oil
Jonah in the belly of the whale
Noah in the ark with every animal
Cain pouring out the blood of Abel

Moses in the basket on the river
like gods ascending from the earth
no man ascended without descending
born from above into new birth

even to the Son of Man
the first fruits of resurrection

42. disciples of honor

there's a low road to heaven
and a high road to hell
pray God's will be done
and I wish you well
you're in control
with hands on the wheel
there's a way in the valley
that turns weakness into steel

we are known through eternity
from strife we gain power
clothed in grace
as disciples of honor

I pledge my love
all the days of my life
I pledge my soul
to the good and the right
I pledge my heart
to my sisters and brothers
who are joined in the light
and at the end leave with honor

all the days of our lives
we refuse the way of shame
we wish nobody harm
and have no one to blame
our high calling will be done
pure eyes now glow
in the darkness we crave good
like waters from the desert flow

43. **slang sanctuary cities of refuge…**

San Fransexo is for the chirpy birds

NO for the voodoo children

Sin City for the gamblin' man

Warshington for the politician

SLUT white salamander jacks

Cashville for the ghettobilly

Hollyweird for the galerians

Miyayo redneck Rivera

Los Faceless for the aliens

Chiraq for the murderer

Habadabah for dearbornistan

Detoilet for the gansta rapper

vampire vultures

flocking together

bats in the cave

you don't wanna go there

11/25/16

3.
the dark red (c)loud of purgatory...

44. purgatory

it was planned
it was biased
it was rigged
it was fixed
it was finished
it was set
it was scammed
it was hexed

she would do anything
she would kill to win
she would drink from the golden goblet
it was filled for her before the end

we all hang together
upon the thinnest threads
in the hangman's noose
with sackcloth on our heads

New York times
Washington Post
and CNN
Newsweek Magazine
the FBI
and DOJ
Soros Smartmatic
the political machine

O God, can it be
it was always a conspiracy?
as I turn around to see
the dark red cloud of purgatory

11/7/16

45. Flannery O'Connor's peacocks

the stars who are ho's
for polito-cause
are like worms and maggots
inside apples
air sucking through
bent noisy straws
grease stains smeared
on dirty windows

I have watched these
actors and pretenders
singers ringers stringers
and big time spenders
like a short story
by Flannery O'Connor
about her troubled peacocks
strutting stumbling over one another

telling everyone
by their lives
that you have no reason
to listen to their lies
you don't have to do
anything that we decide
the only thing you'll ever
have to do is die

rappers who rap nasty
about the welfare whore
while the politician dances
for women's rights and the poor
the crowd went wild
for the free performance

then swarmed to the exits
when she made her appearance

"WE DON'T WANT
TO SHRINK THE VISION,
BUT EXPAND IT
INTO GLOBALISM
WITH NO LINES
AND NO BORDERS
WHERE I AM THE HEAD
OF THE NEW WORLD ORDER!"

11/8/16

73

46. polls are for telephone repair men and dancers

I climbed down the telephone pole
and the old guy on Park Avenue said,
"my neighbor across the street
just died last night."

"oh gee, sorry to hear that!"
"well..." I joked, "are you going
to the polling station
to vote Trump for him?"

"ah, no...I just got back from there,
but I'm not gonna tell you how I voted."

"that's ok I don't mind telling you
that I voted for Trump, but it doesn't matter
because he won't win in California anyway.
the polls are all in Hillary's favor here." I say.

"I hear that polls are for
telephone repair men and dancers...
no matter who you vote for
nobody is happy in the end." he answered.

"well, that's the way it's always been!
wouldn't it be funny if we stole
the vote in California for Trump?
Hillary would go thump!"

I climbed into my truck,
and looked across the street.
the guy who died had a sign on his lawn.
it said: 'Write in Tony Flores for Mayor'
tough luck if Tony and Hillary lose
only by one vote!

11/8/16

74

47. God wants me to write this poem today

they say it is
all about the
numbers

1 to 9
0 is nothing

and you know
I think they are right
the bible has numbers
the numbers have
meaning

1 to 9
0 is space

they are as simple
as they are hard
numbers expand
and implode inward

1 to 9
0 is a circle

God says
count the number
of the beast...
like 666
is 9
(6+6+6
is 18
1+8
is 9)

1 to 9
0 is empty

Lucifer climbed
to the highest
number
the highest
number
is 9
9 is the
devil's number
the devil's number
is 9.

oh my darling,
oh my darling, Clementine
you are lost and gone forever
and your shoes were number 9

God is 1
G*O*D is O*N*E
he's the ruler
of the servant
kingdom
the lowest
number is
one
God wants me
to write this
poem today.
I wrote this poem
on 11/9/2016
and that is 2
and 2 means
witness

1 to 9
0 is forever

numbers are
markers
sign posts
to heaven
to show the road
to walk
and give you
direction

44 is God's judgement
44 is 8
45 is preservation
45 is 9

1 to 9
O keeps spinning

ONE is God and unity
TWO is witness
THREE is completeness
FOUR is earth
FIVE is grace
SIX is man
SEVEN is perfection
EIGHT is a new beginning
NINE is to be divine.

48. cheap exploding Cuban cigar
(inspired by Manny Carballo)

Obama went to Cuba
to pander for the Cuban vote
the Cuban vote in Florida
not to be a lifeboat

America got nothing
he gave away the farm
Castro's brother got everything
he did a lot more harm

Raul released 53 dissidents
of the communist government
then threw them back into prison
after Barack Hussain Obama went

the Cubans who voted for Hillary
were hoping she would keep it open
truth is no one really cared
for a deal that was already broken

the vote he got didn't matter
because the deal was a joke
like a cheap exploding Cuban cigar
it all went up in smoke

11/10/16

49. **here they come**

here they come
torches burning
blood-red blazing
flags desecrated yearning

the old guy
with a liquor store
hugging his precious bottles
hunkered down on the floor

like the world is ending
where everybody dies
agitators sweeping by
with fiercely lit up eyes

burn him in effigy
spear him with a megaphone
I turn on the TV
to watch a Tom and Jerry cartoon

11/10/16

50. how can we endure

how can we endure
all this changing weather
it is a hungry desperate land
when homeless drifters take a stand

where people sleep in gunnysacks
madness slips in through the cracks
where broomsticks, ropes and torches pass
and the walls come down en masse

the vault is set on bankers time
to spill the blood and pour the wine
it's getting hard to close the gate
on this raging flood of hate

11/10/16

51. existential horror skit

there is an
orange monster
with hands
like grenades
with a bright red
horn of fire
and dark
mirror shades

there is a
black monster
with blue hands
on a lever
pulling it
over and over
but he never
seems to tire

it's that cryptic kind
of monster meeting
a wink a nod
a double meaning
that no one else
can know about
"I help you in
you help me out…"

the director shouts, "CUT…
I think we got it!
it's not supposed to make sense,
it's an existential horror skit!"

11/10/16

52. red dog running

there was
an early
moment
when the
electoral map
looked like
a red dog
running

at that moment
I knew that
Donald Trump
was winning

10/11/16

53. Joshua Tree

I brought The Art of The Deal
by our new POTUS elect to read in Joshua Tree
and Sarah and Hailey
grabbed it and started making silly remarks,
as they walked danced and jumped
towards the pool.

"Donald gets up early in the morning..." she reads aloud. "why is
it because Melania snores?"
they both giggle hysterically.

she says, "DAD don't take a picture of us!"

"why not- this will be our last trip to Joshua Tree?
I want to preserve the memory!"

"why, is it because Donald Trump is going to kill us all?"

"yeah, that's right, he is going to use Joshua Tree
to calibrate the nuclear weapons
and test out the rusty old warheads
on the rock formations
on January 20th
and light up the Joshua trees like candles
to celebrate the inauguration!

sweetie, you know mom is selling the place, right?"
just enjoy it while it lasts."

so they jump into the icy cold
November water
suddenly remembering
that they forgot their towels

then click,

the memory freezes in time
and is immortalized in poetry.

10/12/16

54. them diaper babies

how 'bout them diaper babies
ain't they a crime
runnin round the streets
a wavin' they signs

wavin' them hate signs
wavin' they fists
throwin' them tantrums
callin' them protests

them ever doggin' agitators
ain't they flamin' stars
throwin' them rock pertaters
at them police cars

them red doper diaper babies
lookit them spin
when ya stick'em in the hiney
with a safety pin

how to be a diaper baby
if you wanna know it
dig out yer poopie
haul off and throw it

11/13/16

55. the wafflemeister

the say that Trump is waffling
he will keep Obamacare
build a fence instead of a wall
his promises were just hot air

they say he lied to get elected
now he's got to be real
he's still just a democrat
doing the Art of the Deal

I hope that's not his intention
it's a movement and a cause
he'll change our direction
it's just losers grasping straws

Bannon published in Breitbart
Priebus held down the fort
Palin will drill baby drill in ANWR
Sessions will do whatever he wants

no more global warming scares
Jesus is the only one
who can and will destroy this earth
when all our time here is done

he is the most powerful POTUS
this country has ever known
with the Supreme court and both houses
and only the rank and file that he owes

the media and special interests
both parties and the global elite
all went down with smoke and mirrors
in a glorious and miraculous defeat

11/14 16

86

56. **media suicide**

the media is passed out drunk
gas on without the flame
with made up stories and headlines
to repeat their same mistakes again

TRUMP NEEDS OBAMA
HILLARY HAS REALLY WON
A FENCE IS NOT A WALL
WE LICK THE BOOTS OF POLITICIANS

they still work the levers of power
until the inauguration
it's best to keep your head down
in case there is a big explosion

they work with words to shape the lies
it's too much to believe their early wins
someone strikes a match in fury
it ends in the same place it begins

11/15/16

57. the gravity of darkness

a broken peanut shell
of a soul
in the dark side
of the hole
where even a fly
cannot cross
into the light
from the gravity of darkness

failure piled on failure
to embrace redemption
when God held mercy high
to be received by anyone
God send Lazarus
back to tell my brother
the meaning of nothingness
and the shattered dead of forever

11/15/16

58. leading from behind

"Leading From Behind"
is the gay way to go
it's Obama's bumper sticker
his governing White House motto

it's code for doing nothing
and hiding everything you do
spending all the money
and getting nothing new

we want to see behind the curtain
on Scalia, Benghazi, 911…
we want to see the records opened
and know everything he's done

the phony birth certificate
the Indonesian citizenship
the foreign student visas
the Columbia College transcripts

I hope he picks Arpaio
for the head of the DOJ
"JOE DIGS LIKE A DOG IN THE DIRT!"
is what the New York Times will say

he made our country weaker
he bowed down to every world leader
he gave the Muslim brotherhood their power
he turned America into a bottom feeder

that's leading from behind,
leading from behind the veil of lies.

11/16/16

59. the new racism

there is a racialist online code war storming
they don't use nasty terms like rappers
blacks are googles, skypes jews,
asians bings & latinos yahoos
whites are privileged
dog whistles and mouse triggers

the Alt right and the Alt left
are stuck in the mud with a snarl
a snarl they think comes from God
of human decay body mind and soil

a snarl
at the cops
the whores
the rain
the depraved
the flat tires
the voters
the insane
a snarl
on the stairs
on the roof
of the tower
a snarl
that is whispered
from the graves
and the gutter

God made us all in the colors of His own image
male and female He made them
and then said that it was "very good"
God has a feminine side not just masculine

the new racism can never remain
its roots are planted in hidden shame
with an anonymous online name
there is still always a rainbow after the rain

11/17/16

60. **Leonard Cohen's last request**

here comes Lizzy Redcloud Warren,
Chucky Doll Schumer, and Kanye Wessss...
putting out their left foot forward
doing what they do the best

with snake eyes on 2020 prep
like attack dogs barking up Trump's rear
and the Press Corp falling into lockstep
will deliver DJ POTUS 4 more years

the best that 2024 can hope for
is between Ivanka Trump and Kanye West
and "I wish women would hurry up and take over"
like in Leonard Cohen's last request

11/18/16

61. tribulation Trump

is Don John the last president
before Michael stands up?
is that black Harlem preacher right
to call him "Tribulation Trump?"

did he Blorenge on his promise
to put that Crooked Hill in jail?
did he give Barry Hussain a pass
for being an illegal?

is Tribulation Trump
like Zeus the ornithological?
where he turns into a swan
and rapes a little girl

only in Donald's poem
can words rhyme with orange
"a very floppy fish penis:
that piranha has a huge sporange"

if he is the real forerunner
let the real Jesus be your head
and watch out for falling stars
as the moon turns blue to red

so call it John the Bastard
like one who's being sent
to lay out the final groundwork
for Lucifer's big tent Jesus fake event

then I would expect to see Elijah
and Enoch coming next
God is always right on time
and He protects His own elect

11/19/16

93

62. **dodo bird**

Hamilton pontificates & lectures VP on diversity
yet, "seeking only non-whites for roles on Broadway
of all ages between twenty and thirty".
a casting call for those "who rap" like Niki Minaj and Kanye

King George can still be privileged white
but we all wants to cause up quite a stir
with all the founding fathers black as tar
Mike Pence steps right into the role of Aaron Burr

this is more like gay reverse Shakespearean
when he used white men for every female role
and bringing back audience participation
for this leotard madhouse to be back out of control

Hamilton insulted Aaron Burr
And Arron Burr took the shot,
"this play is scripturally inaccurate
with overacting and an overreaching plot"

asking Mike Pence for his respect
while themselves disrespecting him
with this so-called *kind* heckling badgering
is the reason why they will never win

this brand of electroshock therapy
from this little opportunistic c r y b a b y
went the way of the dodo bird, my friend
somewhere back in ancient history

11/20/16

63. Harry Reid's cowboy poetry slam

do the dirty Harry
and kill the filibuster
like the cowboy poetry
up in Elko Nevadar
he got punched in the eye
by a blackjack dealer
wore dark sunglasses
that could see into the future

first Beowulf killed Grendel
then he killed his mother
then he went for the dragon
with his python colt revolver

Harry tried to kill the Bunny's
at the Moonlight Ranch
so's he could pry out the deed
from their cold dead hands
he shot at the Bundy's
in a shady land grab
to deal in the Chinese
with a cheatin' poker hand

then he shot at the dealer
and shot off his ear
and he shot up the stage
shot holes in Shakesteer
then he shot Beowulf in the back
and took the dragons gold
said "if'n ya lose yer fillerbuster
then it's a gittin' time to fold!"

11/21/16

64. the revolt of the dyke brigade

to the archetype villains of Santa Sangre
Mrs. Robinson and Nancy Pelosi
Loretta Lynch and Huma Abedin
Boxer and Streisand Barbie doll babies

the Monster from the Blue Lagoon
destroyed in a gale force wind
like Athena Ishtar the goddess Ceto
it's the wreck of Hillary Roddam Clinton

the Revolt of The Dyke Brigade
like the song John Fahey played
on a Bacon and Day Senorita
for the long lost feeling of Americana

suffrage came from Republicans
democrats were the KKK
the democrats fought hard to keep slavery
the republicans swept it all away

Clinton Foundation pay to play
the same old story with a different face
to call good evil and evil good
well God finally played an ace

11/22/16

65. billygoat Billy

Billy's jumping up and down
the oval orifice makes him sing
feeding time is back around
a goat will eat most anything

he sings a goat song to wash away
the fantasia darkness of yesterday
he thanks goat god for a his new hay
and for everything to go his way

but Billy won't be chewing here
Billy won't be chewing there
Billy lost more than just teeth
he won't be chewing anywhere

the feed barn door was locked up tight
but he kept chewing on the nob
it happened the farmhouse burned last night
and the dogs ate cooked up farmer Bob

11/22/16

66. tit for tat

God gave Judas the money bag
politicians gave 30 pieces of silver
it's hanging in the balance scale
between betrayal and eternal treasure

it's always been a two-edged sword
God was always tit for tat
remember John the Baptist's head
is Don Corleone going to the mat?

tit for tat
this for that
the universal battle
between good and evil

God killed the Pharaoh son's
Satan killed God's chosen one's
the angel of death passed over
Rachel weeping for her children

Jacob stole Esau's name
Esau went and did the same
Herod was an Edomite
who became the Jews king

when Herod sat upon the throne
they shouted, "Voice of God not a man!"
the angel struck him so he died
and worms ate him from inside

Hussain/John were meant to be
give God the praise don't get upset
God is doing the greatest job
and he isn't finished yet >

11/23/16

67. dear Hillary letter from Saul Alinsky...

dear Hillary dear Hillary
friction and heat
maneuver and bait
attack and defeat
hide all your numbers
if you're starting out small
show only your power
and soon they will fall

never go outside
from experience to confusion
it'll cause fear and retreat
and collapse communication
but always go outside
the enemies own lines
and cause them desertion
by truth mixed with lies

make the enemy live
by their own book of rules
you can kill them with this
like all Christian fools
mockery ridicule and satire
is your most powerful weapon
it infuriates opposition
and causes reaction

a good tactic is one
your people enjoy
they'll keep on doing it
create their own to employ
if it drags on too long
it becomes stale old news
it's all about movement
on the path that you choose

keep up the pressure
keep the threat terrifying
keep pushing it through
keep the act death defying
dear Hillary dear Hillary
if you follow these well
then hell will be heaven
and heaven will be hell

signed,
truly from the Devil's servant Alinsky

PS: say hi to my baby boy Obama

11/26/16

68. dear Saul letter from Hillary Clinton...

dear Sauly dear Sauly
my secret love
we'll change the world
from below and above
mold it in our image
of goddess and god
and rule it with a fist
like a brass iron rod

we'll dedicate it to Lucifer
our great organizer
and lead the useful idiots
right into his lair
I can't wait to see you
when you get back from Asia
you can show me the meaning
of a junket to exotica

signed,
love from your adoring admirer Hillary

PS: I'll be waiting for you at the San Fransexo Hilton

11/26/16

69. the green flame

drunk on green beer
in staggers Jill Stein
to make the deal go queer
hot flares up her behind
she rattles the iron chains
head down for the blast
with her army of paid trolls
she strikes up a match

the green flame burns
the color of money
the color of envy
the color of tyranny
the color of misery
the color of the party
the green flame is poison
the black smoke is integrity

what she has been up to
is not that hard to see
a strong arm attempt
to bilk the democrat party
she's asking for money
with a no refund clause
to repo our republic
and torch our electoral college

but why would Hill join Jill
after she conceded?
is it to hide the voter fraud
that she herself did?
she sees indictment coming
wants to cover up her tracks
as the green flame is burning
she needs to fill in the cracks?

Hillary can't believe Americans
are so stupid to vote for Trump
Jill says it's the Russians
in a hackers data dump
the party is in shambles
they need money and direction
before they explode like fireworks
into a leaderless insurrection

I say let hippie Jill have her fun
the democrats are just plain dumb
let her bleed them all dry
and then let's watch her run
she can take all their money
for all anybody cares
the green flame the green drain
watch it all just disappear

11/28/16

70. Mutt Romney Blues #2

5, 6, 7, 8
now boss Donald Trump went for a flight
pulled up on a runway gate
tied me down to the tail of his jet
boss I howled, this just don't seem right

please master boss!
give me a pass
Ow Ow Ahoo!
please master boss
don't kick my ass
Ow Ow Ahoo!

dog in the day, doggin' all night
where this will end I don't know
my bark was worse than my bite
poor Mutt's got to buckle up and go

Oh Mr. boss
please cut me down
I won't spread this tale around
all those mean things I said about you
no one believed they were true
Ow Ow Ahoo!
,

he had to fly, sure not flyin'
poor Mutt, he really had a ride
he had to fly, sure not flyin"
up on the tail here I am tied

hold on Mutt's got to buckle up and go
Ow Ow Ahoo!

11/28/16

71. who is Julian Assange?

did Hillary Clinton's
body double drone
of porno Pamela Anderson
poison our boy Julian
with a spirit cooked vegan sandwich
when she went to meet him
or is he just missing
because they can't stop kissing?

first they cut his internet
when he released the transcripts
of her Goldman Sachs speeches
how loose lips sink ships
then a jet stream was seen
taking off from London
the same kind used by the CIA
for covert operations

he's been missing over 30 days
"Proof of life" everybody says
will it flip the Dead Man's Switch
has Wikileaks been compromised
everybody wants to know!
did the CIA take our hero
and turn WikiLeaks
into useless twaddle?

truth trump's lies
in this new American Revolution
the dissolving of Soros control
the media and the Clinton Corporation
it's a new day shining
another Paul Revere is riding
saying "The White Dragons are coming!
The Globalists are running!"

is it all just a psyop
a fake out and a realignment
is Assange just another agent
who completed an assignment
who gets away with 4 years
of openly screwing the government?
they could have killed him long ago
and made it look like an accident

try to take the longer view
does someone want Armageddon?
you can't trust anything anymore
or anyone but Christ again
the pawns hide behind a face
the queen is laying on the board
the black king moves back a space
and the angel of light is at the door

11/30/16

4.
Merry (C)hristmas and a happy New Year…

72. **God has his own calendar**

God has his own calendar
the 1st day of spring is his new year
not that stone cold day in January
that's frozen solid as an icy river

Christ was born in late September
God calls himself a green fir tree
Jesus was conceived 9 months earlier
so December 25th doesn't bother me

life begins at conception
God with us God as man
when Elizabeth heard Mary's greeting
her baby leaped inside her womb

no one knows the hour or day
when the Son of Man will return
all we know is how time slips away
and we never will have time to burn

God has his own calendar
hanging on his wall
and this month has a picture
of wise men giving gifts to all

12/1/16

73. demon

that howdy howdy Harlem preacher
says the son of Satan's long-legged demon

will enter into the son of Hitler
at the President's inauguration

from the way I've seen it rave
it's a nasty scratchy scary one

but that's not funny it's kinda grave
I hope the DJ's a not a hip hop Christian

with God's angelic firewall to save
and the blank 'white label' of protection

12/2/16

74. no king but king Jesus

we have no king but King Jesus
no king but King Jesus
no king but King Jesus
the Lord of the universe

we have no king but King Jesus
no king but King Jesus
no king but King Jesus
to Him I pledge allegiance

we have no king but King Jesus
no king but King Jesus
no king but King Jesus
over my heart He reigns

75. Mary had a baby

Mary had a baby
O Mary had a baby
and his name was Jesus
O what a sight it was

Mary had a baby
O Mary had a baby
He was born in a manger
O what a sight it was

a gleam was spotted in the sky
a star shining down from on high
like a light beam from God's eye
on His newborn Son

the shepherds came to see him
the shepherds came to see him
they left their sheep behind them
O what a sight it was

then there came three wise men
then there came three wise men
with gold myrrh and frankincense
O what a sight it was

as baby Jesus got older
Mary's excitement grew
she knew he came from the Father
and longed to see what God would do

Mary had a baby
O Mary had a baby
and his name was Jesus
O what a sight it was

76. let's go America!

let's go America!
lift yourself off the ground
let's hold our banner high
and wipe away the frown
you flew us to the moon
you landed us on mars
let's give it all we've got
and reach out past the stars

keep on trying
keep on trying
you never know what we can do
keep on trying
keep on trying
and we're going to make it through

let's go America!
raise old glory high
be strong America!
let all her colors fly
we'll make it in the end
and let our freedom ring
east to west hand in hand
everybody sing!

life to America!
it is the greatest land
life to America!
God blessed her by his hand
through many trials
hurricanes and war
they make her stronger
for evermore.

77. manual carburetor

we took the supervisor
out for a beer after 35 years of working
for the company.

we took him to that bar where they caught the postal killer
Richard Hilbun calmly watching sports TV,
the Centerfield Sports Bar...
back in the day I played here as well with the Homeless Drifters.

Manny the Cuban...let go between Thanksgiving and Christmas
the Company Frontier ripped 1000 managers in the State.
(I guess nature balancing itself out with the Carrier move...)

he was sitting beside Irene, the sales lady and the other guys had
not arrived yet. Manny says, "I think in gonna leave cause no
one is going to come"

"not yet, I just saw all the guys in the yard and they are on their
way over!" he was happy to hear that so he came over and gave
me a hug.

"you know I still have your poetry books and music cd's in my
car..." he told me.

"well I'll make sure you get the next one. you know you did me a
big favor Manny you saved my butt when that witch targeted me
and tried to get rid of me. I want you to know I'll never forget it."

"ah no big deal man it wasn't all that hard to push downhill..."

just then, the guys came sauntering through the door.
there were the 3 Brian's,
Bryan the Gambler,
Brian the Casanova,
Brian the hot head.

there was Don the good-natured know it all,
and Lee the Asian gang banger family man,
then finally Beau the FMLA troublemaker.

I bought Manny his beer and ordered a water "what you don't
drink? are you a priest?   are you AA or something?"

"no, I used to drink, never had a problem with it.
I just decided to quit and haven't touched a drop in 30 years.
I'm kind of the anti-Bukowski that way!"

(I decided to wait for that great day
to have a glass of wine with Jesus;
"but I say to you, I will not drink of this fruit of the vine from
now on until that day when I drink it new with you in my
Father's kingdom.")

"so if you end up having to move back to Cuba you sure will
have a lot of nice old classic cars to choose from," I said.

"No! you know those cars may look good from the pictures you
see on TV, but they aren't any good. A 57 Chevy might have a
Volga engine and a modified 49 Ford drivetrain. You can't get
original parts there and everything is scrounged! I will say
though, if I ever got stranded anywhere with a broken down car,
I would want a Cuban mechanic along…they can piece anything
together and make it work!"

I guess that's why Fidel Castro's funeral procession Jeep broke
down mid ceremony and his soldiers had to push Castro's ashes
into his grave…a picture perfect ending for that murderous
communist dictator in his tiny little coffin...

12/4/16

115

78. **America is Christian**

the sun hits America
with self-sustaining light
it generates variety
and intensity of life
it's not a deep freeze
or a land of desert heat
like icy Russian Siberia
or the waterless Middle East

America is great
America is blessed
America is exceptional
America is prosperous
America is free
America is sovereign
in God we trust
America is Christian

everything grows here
the seasons regulate
the mother of invention
unique in every State
energy and beauty
fisheries and farms
many hate and envy her
and try to do her harm

like Andrew Jackson's KKK
Roosevelt the communist
Carter the wet noodle president
Nixon the criminal alchemist
Clinton the sex crazed rapist
Bush New World Order globalism
Obama the Muslim terrorist
Trump for preservation

911 was a turning point
for the Satanic Verses of WW3
fighting everyone on every front
"with those who don't think like me"
there is good and there is evil
Christ Jesus is the only way
judgement begins with his people
America humble yourselves and pray

12/5/16

79. #Gore

why is Trump meeting with Gore?
that deadbeat global warming whore
who sells carbon credits like snake oil cure
while his jet pollutes the atmosphere!

is Ivanka trying to be the Czar?
to that hoax of a global warming scare
to punish the non-payers everywhere
and make America pick up the fare...

Vladimir Putin really knows the score,
he called it for what it was for
just a fraud and nothing more
to stop oil drilling and spending on fur.

it's probably HAARP controlling the weather
to make the climate changelings look better
and the chemtrail jets salting the air
to jack the rainclouds like a poisonous flare

in the guise of Lieberman-Warner
a bill not to make the climate more secure
but to cap and trade and sell out our welfare
and rain down more pollution in the future.

12/7/16

80. coconut oil

once I was old but now I'm young
it's the coconut oil the coconut oil
so I wrote this song and this is how it sung
it's the coconut oil the coconut oil
take a little out and your rub it on your head
it's a coconut oil the coconut oil
make shiny and bright what used to be dead

coconut oil
give it a chance
make you jump right up
and do a little dance

the banana boat was moving slow
they use coconut oil to make it go
coconut oil well there's no other way
if you want to live both happy and gay

call 1-800 for your order today
use your credit card cause that's how you pay
it keeps on coming it will never stop
read the fine print to see what you got

81. the Constitution

there's a battle etched in the cave
between the slave and the free
to laws of nature and of nature's God
that are self-evident for all to see

if you crawl into the lion's den
to play with the little baby lion
and the mother tears you limb from limb
they would say '*WTF was wrong with him*?'

they wouldn't blame the mother lion
for its natural right of protection
and declaw all lions everywhere
by denying de lion de 2nd Amendment

the Constitution is your protection
with the Bill of Rights and Declaration
it kills progressivism in its tracks
as well as sharia and globalism

since the founding of this country
it's nature's way to prefer its own
with the right to be self-governed
and nature's God sitting on the throne

12/8/16

82. I don't like writing poems

John calls to say hello
and tells me his studio
is almost back up and running
after a computer crash
now he can start working
on a new project for Showtime
called 'The Affair'

I tell him how sick I have been the last week
off work and laid up in bed and coughing, dizzy, delirious…

a restricted call comes in and I ignore it,
after we finish talking we hang up
it comes in again so I answer it.

"hello is this Eddy Duhan?" says a kids voice trying to sound
like a grown up.

(now I'm getting prank calls
from my daughter and her
friends at her high school...)

"maybe, what's this about?" I here girls laughing in the
background. "who is this? did Sarah put you up to it?"

"uh nooo, I'm Robert Stant, do you like to write poems?"

"NO, not at all, absolutely not!"

I hear him say, "HEY we got the wrong Eddy! this guy doesn't
like writing poems" more laughter and he hangs up.

I almost expect a call back, but nothing...
they must have been rushing between classes.

and then I get a call from my wife
saying someone stole Sarah's lunch from her locker,
and she was going to bring her another one,
what a world!

so I download a farting ringtone app on to my phone,
tried it, have a laugh, and uninstalled it right afterward.

when Sarah got home I said, "so who is Robert Stant? was it one
of your friends making prank phone calls, asking me if I like to
write poetry?"

"don't know what tour talking about, maybe it was someone
from Donald Trump's team."

12/15/16

83. Arab spring

Syria wanted Russia
to build a pipeline
so the Arabs and the globalists
all lost their minds
Obama hired ISIS
to overthrow Assad
and gave them the weapons
they needed for the job

they're falling like dominoes
and called it the Arab spring
it's not democracy and freedom
it's about the changing of regime

they ran guns through Benghazi
"but what does it matter now"
they gave Iran blood money
to bring the middle-east down
Hillary killed Gaddafi
laughed "we came we saw he died"
this is Obama's legacy;
'the destroyer from inside'

They stopped him in Aleppo
now Obama is out of time
there is nothing he can do
but watch it all unwind
so much wasted money
so many wasted lives
it time to flush away
the nightmare of our times

12/16/16

84. you can get most everything you need
(to the tune: 'You Can't Always Get What You Want' by The Rolling Stones)

I saw Trump today at the rally
he had the big crowd in his hand
I knew he was gonna win the election
with the people who were there to hear his plan

you can get most everything you need
you can get most everything you need
you can get most everything you need
with Trump and his team ready to take the lead

I went on to twitter and the internet
to see WikiLeaks and Veritas
singing, "we're finally getting the truth revealed to us
and throwing corrupt politicians underneath the bus"

you can get most everything you need
you can get most everything you need
you can get most everything you need
with Trump and his team ready to take the lead

I watched every 'Thank You Tour'
in every swing state that he won
I watched it shining like old glory
and man, it was lookin' pretty fun
it was time to raise out flag high again
the colors of our red white and blue
I sung my song about never seeing it burn again
yeah, and it said one word to me, and that was "true"
I said to him

you can get most everything you need
you can get most everything you need
you can get most everything you need
with Trump and his team ready to take the lead

12/17/16

124

85. the Harry Reid memorial nuclear waste repository

in the wild of Yucca Mountain Nev-AD-a
70k metric tons of waste will find its home
they paid the billions in fees a long time ago
and got nothin' but a spaghetti western poem

now Trump can soon resurrect and revive it
to try and get this monkey off our back
it's a good place to store radioactive waste
A state that went and voted democrat

Congress approved it back in the 80's
Harry Reid has always blocked the route
but since he went and killed the filibuster
he lost his power and now he is out

with his tinfoil hat shining on his head
he keeps on shootin' off his mouth
with insults and neurosis at the Donald
in his classic Woody Allen styled nervous bout

the Harry Reid memorial nuclear waste repository
a good place to hatch the eggs of Carnosaur
and awake Godzilla's monster pod with radioactivity
to wreak havoc carnage and explosions right outside his door

12/17/16

125

86. from the news desk of Christopher Sign at KNXV

it was supposed to be a secret meeting
except for one journalist who caught a glimpse
the Secret Service told everyone to put away their phones and to
take no pictures
while Bill Clinton sneaked over the runway to pow wow with
Loretta Lynch

Clinton waited at the airport Monday night for Lynch to arrive
the next morning
then boarded her plane for a 30-minute hiphop jibjive meeting
it happened on the private tarmac used for take offs and landings
thank goodness that Christopher Sign caught wind of their shady
dealings

so here is my shout out to Phoenix KNXV-TV
and my shout down to the FBI who tried to disallow the
journalists to photograph the meeting
now Loretta is trying to save face on the news channels every
morning
as her power and influence dwindles and her job prospects are all
receding

12/18/16

87. a 911 faker an unfaithful elector

Christopher Suprun
Benedict Arnold
Texas dog meat
one unfaithful elector
a so called first responder
to fight the fire
at the Pentagon
but really a 911 faker
dressed up
in stolen valor
like a purple heart
pinned on a liar

Trump probably didn't want your vote anyway…

12/19/16

88. they say Trump is backing off

they say Trump is backing off
on Russian aggression
they say Trump is backing off
on lock her up
they say Trump is backing off
on make Mexico pay
they say Trump is backing off
on drain the swamp
they say Trump is backing off
on too many things to say

they say the Republican establishment
is taking over
in the Trump administration
that it truly is the New World Order

they say China and Russia
are now ascending
that we're afraid of confrontation
it's like we have Stockholm syndrome
the shipping lanes
in the China Sea
the occupation of the Crimea
the Ukrainian thing is personal to me

Trump will never save the world
and Christ is our only hope
but I prefer his brand of poison
to the globalist hangman's rope
to be on the Tower of Babel
and to control the top tier
and to be the all seeing eye
on the pyramid of the dollar

12/22/16

89. **BOOM!**

we finally have a President
who is telling us what they are:
"Radical Islamic Terrorists"
the same thing they have been telling us
about themselves forever

"Allahü Akbar! the Muslim assassin yelled!
We are the ones who pledged Bai'a
to Mohammed on the terms of jihad
as long as we live."

we are at war
with fundamental Islamic terrorism
there is only one equation
for the final solution

BOOM goes Mecca BOOM goes Medina
Boom Shakalaka Nagasaki Hiroshima
it's not like we haven't done it once before
or at least make them think we'll do it once more
just kidding

12/23/16

90. **give Trump a chance**

everybody's talking about
Hillary, Billery, chillary, killery
all the way to zillary
globalism, theisim
thisism, thatism
party schisim, going to prison

all we are saying
is give Trump a chance
all we are saying
is give Trump a chance

everybody's talking about
millionaires billionaires
trillionaires zillionaires
buying shares, cold stares,
liberal tears, safety pins
crybabies, who cares

all we are saying
is give Trump a chance
all we are saying
is give Trump a chance

everybody's talking about
fox news, red shoes, blue blues
oil drilling, global warming
repealing and replacing
art of dealing,
swamp draining, vote stealing

all we are saying
is give Trump a chance
all we are saying
is give Trump a chance
everybody out...   *12/24/16*

91. the old gunfighter

I have been
sick coughing hacking and weary
with no desire
for a long time
to pick up
my banjolele pistole
or my 4 or 5 string banjo Winchesters
or my ukulele derringer
my classical Smith and Wesson heater
or my steel string acoustic 6 shooter
or my electric machine gun telecaster
or my hollow body long shot repeater

I force myself
to pull out the banjolele pistole
struggle to load it GCEA
'Guns Capped Edwardo's Arsenal'
and for some reason
I always play this instrumental first...
'A Hard Road to Travel'
by John Fahey
then,
'Come Thou long expected Jesus'
'When the Saints go Marching in'
'Joy to the World'
'The First Noel'
'Silent Night'

then I try and sing/recite something
an old Mason Williams rewrite
of 'J. Edgar Swoop'
changed to 'D.J. Trump'

after that I dredge up an old obscure song,
'Ghosts on the Prairie' and take a shot…

"we drove the cattle North
from the Mexican border
the wind was hot and thirsty
and drank up all the water
winter came too early
caught out in the storm
stranded in the canyon
just trying to keep warm
well Cookie caught sick
died on Christmas Day
so we just crossed some sticks
for the headstone on his grave
left a cold empty feeling
burning in our minds
singing Jesus won't you help us
through these times…"

I fizzle out like a dud firework
before I make it to the chorus,
and put the smoldering banjolele pistole
back in its holster

I feel like the old gunfighter
recovering in the Unforgiven
or The Good the Bad and the Ugly
I break a sweat shake and shiver…

12/25/16

92. Pokémon Go

Pokébo's going for the revenge kill
he's up against one punch Pokétrump
he'll prove to all that his paper trail
will pokeball his legacy into the dump
then white out all the residual damage
that he signed over the last eight years
in his trick room with his toxic spikes
he lies in wait before he disappears

if this is taking the high road
I'd hate to see him take the low
as he goes out into the world
to play cheaters Pokémon Go

he takes a sucker punch at wild Putimon
tries to steal Pokétrumps lucky eggs
he throws out a rapid spin temper tantrum
kicks Bibi Pokémon in the Pokidex
can't wait to see his gym hit zero
he's such a big embarrassment
with his history of nasty plot battles
he's the real energy ball Jellicent

12/29//16

93. the Manchurian

the Obummer's aren't budging
they got another house in town
and left behind a garden
of steel rock and stone
trying to lock in their legacy
in a house they built on sand
glued together with executive orders
but it will never stand

like the angry evicted renters
pouring cement down the pipes
pulling out the wires
and smashing all the lights
cutting smoke detectors
breaking all the glass
until the Marshall comes
and kicks'em in the ass

Trump is a master builder
he will bulldoze down the garden
replace it with a putting green
and blow the house of cards in
get rid of every trace
with the smallest gust of wind
undo the damage that he did
with his telephone and pen

I called George Bush years ago
to stop the inauguration
I said he is the Manchurian
and not even a US citizen
they said "you won't get help from us"
and hung up the telephone
so I never listened to him once
finish a sentence that he spoke

1/1/17

134

94. everything is going to be okay

build the wall
build the wall
build the wall
and make Mexico pay

(chorus)
if you keep your promise
if you keep your promise
if you keep your promise
everything is going to be okay

lock her up
lock her up
lock her up
and throw the key away

repeal and replace
repeal and replace
repeal and replace
ObamaCare cannot stay

drain the swamp
drain the swamp
drain the swamp
it's time for a brand new way

1/2/17

95. pure comedy gold

pure comedy gold
dripping off the tree
Obama redefining sex
as the male hysterectomy
it's hot to be a chickdude
to mansplain the masculine
and forget about John Wayne
by rejecting the paradigm

so what is it to be a man
in this day and age
is it to be a snowflake
a zero testosterone gauge?
at least the Texas judge
had enough common sense
to bitch slap Obama down
and the tranny on the fence

1/4/17

96. John Lewis
(sung in the style of the Reverend Gary Davis)

John Lewis is a sensitive trigger
he marched with King from Selma town
they say'd he became a civil rights leader
when they hit him on de head and knocked him down

(chorus)
John Lewis......John Lewis
hit'em on the head and they knocked him down
John Lewis......John Lewis
ran for Congress when he got up off the ground

he say'd ain't gwine down de inauguration
he say'd the same thing to George Bush too
he say'd they ain't gwine be my president's
blamin' hanging chads and Russian ditty wah do

President elect say'd yo town is burnin'
you got to spend mo time fixin' what's fallin' apart
instead of complainin' about de' lection
not just talk talk talkin' but let's make a new start

John Lewis....old John Lewis
ran for Congress in Atlanta town

1/16/17

97. Luke 15

Obama pardoned dangerous criminals
on his way out the White House door
like Tony Montana and Bradley Manning
left bodies scattered across the floor

Loretta Lynch signed a secret order
to give away secrets from the NSA
to secure her cloak and dagger future
when out of power and hidden away

they remind me of that unjust steward
who changed everything in his favor
where even Jesus was amazed
at his manipulation and shrewd behavior

1/19/17

98. inauguration invitation letter from Donald J. Trump

Make America Great Again

Eddy,

you believed in our movement when no one else did.
you are the reason we will Make America Great Again!

which is why I'd love you to be there when we make it official,
and I'm humbly sworn in as your president.

the entire world will be watching that day. but let me be clear:
they will not be watching me. they will be watching us.

they will be watching a new chapter in American history unfold.
they will be watching a movement of free people reclaim their
independence. they will be watching us unite as one people,
saluting one American flag, ready to deliver real change for our
country.

this isn't my inauguration. it's ours.

when I raise my right hand to take the Oath of Office, I will be
doing it in honor of the forgotten men and women of our
country, who banded together to usher in a historic victory last
November.

Eddy: I'll be doing it for you.

I hope to see you there on this historic day.

thank you,

Donald J. Trump
President-Elect of the United States

1/20/17

5.
mine eyes have seen the glory
of the (c)oming of the Lord...

99. I looked for someone among them who would build up the wall...

there is a conspiracy of her princes within her
like a roaring lion tearing its prey;
they devour people, take treasures and precious things
and make many widows within her.

her priests do violence to my law and profane my holy things;
they do not distinguish between the holy and the common;
they teach that there is no difference
between the unclean and the clean;
and they shut their eyes to the keeping of my Sabbaths,
so that I am profaned among them.

her officials within her are like wolves tearing their prey;
they shed blood and kill people to make unjust gain
her prophets whitewash these deeds for them
by false visions and lying divinations.

they say, 'this is what the Sovereign Lord says'
—when the Lord has not spoken.
the people of the land practice extortion and commit robbery;
they oppress the poor and needy and mistreat the foreigner,
denying them justice.

I looked for someone among them who would build up the wall
and stand before me in the gap on behalf of the land
so I would not have to destroy it, but I found no one.
so I will pour out my wrath on them and consume them
with my fiery anger, bringing down on their own heads
all they have done, declares the Sovereign Lord.

Ezekiel 22

100. **I hope in your mercies**

bad habits entangle me like snares
I sink to the very depths of evil
I rejoice at being bound
so daily the enemy gives me new shackles

I appear to be robed in the beautiful clothes
but my soul is entangled in shameful thoughts
to all who might see I appear composed
but inside I am filled with bitter loss

how pitiful I am in my daily repentance
for it has no firm foundation.
every day I lay a stone on the building
and with my own hand cause its destruction

I hope in Thy mercies I fall at Thy feet
lead my soul out of iniquity
may a ray of light shine in my mind
Lord Jesus Christ have mercy on me

101. **legacy**

the pureness of the eyes now glow
our highest calling will be done
in the darkness we crave the good
like light shining from the sun

all the days of my life
I refuse the way of shame
do no harm to anyone
and have no one else to blame

we gain power from strife
we are known through eternity
clothed in gratitude and love
at the end we leave our legacy

102. **the harbor** *(from the Union CD)*

our fathers have entered the harbor
but we are still wandering adrift at sea
even though I feel so lost
yet in my soul, I know you're here with me

let waves of grace fall over me
washing me clean of every stain
let waves of grace fall over me
rescuing me again and again
guide me to the harbor

when I was young I sailed the sea
like a dream inside a dream
with joy and fear I drifted free
toward the sunsets fading gleam

103. **Prayer of Jonah** *(from the Union CD)*

out of my distress I called to the Lord
and he answered me
from the womb of Sheol
I cried for help
and you heard my voice
you cast me into the deep
into the heart of the sea
and the flood enveloped me
all your breakers and your billows
passed over me

then I said I am banished from your sight
how will I again look upon your holy temple
the waters surged around me up to my neck
the deep enveloped me
seaweed wrapped around my head

I went down to the roots of the mountains
to the land whose bars closed behind me forever
but you brought my life up from the pit
O Lord, my God

my prayer came to thee
when I was wasting away
with a heart of thanksgiving
that which I vowed I will pay

my prayer came to thee
when I was wasting away
with a heart of thanksgiving
that which I vowed I will pay
that which I vowed I will pay

holy holy holy holy
holy holy holy holy

those who worship worthless idols
abandon hope abandon mercy
but I with thankful voice
will sacrifice to you to you my God

holy holy holy holy
holy holy holy holy

in love you heard my cry
in love you answered me
in kindness and mercy
you're with me
in love you heard my cry
in love you answered me
in kindness and mercy
you're with me
you're with me
you're with me

104. Psalm 55

listen to my prayer O God
hear my cry for help
I am filled with troubles
my heart pounds in my chest

had I wings like a dove
I'd fly away and rest
I would fly far away
to the quiet wilderness

give your burdens to the Lord
He will bear them for you
the deceiver shall fade away
but you shall not be moved

evening and morning and noon
I cry in my distress
I have escaped unharmed
because you heard my voice

105. song of restoration

out of the gulf into the glory
Father my soul cries out to be lifted
dark is the world and dismal the story
in your sunlit world I stormily drifted

Savior, at peace in purity
shape me in loves security

I have done many things shameful
O Father my heart is sore with aching
help me to ache as much as I need
You are the potter, restoring, remaking

proud of the form you gave this soul
down in the dust I began to nestle
poured you no wine drank deep dishonor
Lord, you broke and mended your vessel

106. conspiracy

do not call conspiracy
everything this people
calls a conspiracy
do not fear what they fear,
and do not dread it.
the Lord Almighty is the one
you are to regard as holy,
he is the one you are to fear,
he is the one you are to dread.
He will be a holy place;
for both Israel and Judah he will be
a stone that causes people to stumble
and a rock that makes them fall.
and for the people of Jerusalem
he will be a trap and a snare.
many of them will stumble;
they will fall and be broken,
they will be snared and captured

Isaiah 8

151

107. from Zachariah

I lifted up my eyes and looked
I lifted up my eyes and saw
I lifted up my eyes again
to the mercies of the Lord

the Lord God shall blow a trumpet
His arrows shall go forth as lightening
He shall stand upon his holy mountain
all his praises we shall sing

there shall be truth and peace
and the Lord shall be our God
there shall be no wickedness
in the house of the Lord

108. thank you

thank you for the sun
You give to keep us warm
like a coat to a weary traveler
heading into the storm
You give us what we need
to make it back to you
thank you Lord eternal
for everything you do

Lord I want to worship you
like I was created to do

all the storehouse of creation
with the stars of heaven
the good things of the earth
and the gifts that you've given
thank you for your love
thank you for your kindness
thank you for your cross
You share your life with us

109. Isaiah 30

the light of the moon shall be as the sun
when the Lord heals the stroke of your wound
and you shall have a song in the night
and the sun will shine seven times bright

in returning you shall be saved
in affliction and distress
quietness shall be your strength
when you hear His glorious voice

long for Him for the Lord is God
and He waits to show compassion
for He longs to be gracious to you
to deliver you from the lion

110. **this is Jesus**

they wagged their heads,
and hurled abuse.
this is Jesus,
king of the Jews.
He saved others,
but he cannot save Himself.
if you are the Son of God,
then come down from the cross..

this is Jesus,
truly this was the Son of God

darkness fell,
across the land at noon.
the veil of the temple,
was torn in two.
the earth shook
and rocks split apart,
many saints came up,
from out of their tombs.

this is Jesus,
truly this was the Son of God

the angel of the Lord,
rolled away the stone.
His garment was white as snow.
He said do not be afraid,
come and see where he was laid
He is not here
He has risen from the grave

this is Jesus,
truly this was the Son of Go

111. **I hope you will be ready**

I hope you will be ready when Jesus comes again.
is he your one desire is he your closest friend?
or when you stand before him will he tell you to depart?
it will happen all too quickly for the changing of your heart.

I hope you will be ready
and I hope I will be too
I hope we will be ready
because I want to be with you

like a thief in the night he'll be coming around.
is your house in order the way you'd like it to be found?
or will he find you sleeping instead of standing on your guard?
have you hidden what he's given is it buried in the yard?

I hope you will be ready when Jesus comes again.
is he your one desire is he your closest friend?
when you hear that last trumpet sound the winds of change have
blown,
you'll be left to face the music and reap what you have sown!

11/4/80

112. Deborah's song

a revelation was made
when the people were made willing
praise ye the Lord
I will sing a psalm to the king

O Lord in thy going forth
the earth quaked dropped dew from heaven
the clouds dropped water
and the mountains were shaken

awake awake awake
arise and utter a song
rise up for this *is* the day
which the Lord has delivered us on

let all Thine enemies perish
and they that love him shall be
as the going forth of the sun
in his strength and glory

113. living water

look at the water
the blue water
falling down
the mountainside
see the water
the crystal water
flow like visions
down from the skies

it's like the water
the living water
flowing down
from the glorious throne
it's like the water
the clear water
pouring out
from Moses stone

Jesus is the living water
the living water is the word
the word came down from the Father
to fill the souls of those who heard

114. I see Jesus

I see Jesus
in the promise of Abraham
I see Jesus
in the burning tree
I see Jesus
in the furnace with the children
I see Jesus
when he died for me

I see Jesus
in baby Moses on the river
I see Jesus
crossing the Red Sea
I see Jesus
walking on the water
I see Jesus
when he set me free

He brings back
love from the grave
He brings back
life and redemption
and great power to save

Jesus in the lion's den
Jesus in Noah's ark
Jesus in Jonah's whale
Jesus in my heart

115. the sower went out to sow

the sower went out to sow
the sower went out to sow
the sower went out to sow one day
and the seeds fell on the ground

help me Lord to know your word
help me Lord to know your word
and give me ears to hear
what needs to be heard

one fell by the wayside
one fell by the way
one fell by the wayside
and the birds of heaven came

one fell on the rocky place
one fell on the rocky place
and before it even had begun
It was scorched and dried by the sun

one e fell on the thorny ground
one fell in the thorns
and they grew up and choked it down
and did not bring its corn

And others fell on good earth
some fell on the good earth
And they gave their increase
when the sower went out to sow the word

116. Psalm 91

He that dwells in the help of the Highest
shall dwell under the shelter of heaven
He shall say you are my helper
my God and I will hope in him

for he delivers from the snare of the hunters
from the troublesome arrows and slings
He shall overshadow you with his shoulders
and you shall trust under his wings

His truth shall cover you with a shield
you shall not be afraid of terror by night
the arrow by day the evil in darkness
calamity at noonday and the evil spirit

a thousand shall fall at your side
and ten thousand at your right
but it shall not come near to you
you shall only see it with your eyes

for You O Lord are my hope
my soul made a refuge of the Most High
no evils shall come upon your dwelling
and no scourge shall draw nigh

for he shall give his angels charge
to keep thee in all your ways
if you dash your foot against a stone
they shall bear you up on their hands

you shalt tread on the serpent
and trample on the lion and dragon
in me hoped and I will deliver him
because he has known my name

he shall call me and I will listen
I am with him in affliction
I will satisfy him with length of days
and show him my salvation

117. **Proverbs 22**

a good name is better than riches
favor is better than silver or gold
rich and poor have this in common
the Lord has made them all

so may your trust be in the Lord
to show you what is right and true
it's pleasant if you keep his word
He will make it known to you

for the Lord loves holy hearts
that speak with grace to the king
the Lord loves holy hearts
the blameless are received by him

the wicked shall reap troubles
but God will help the poor and needy
for the Lord will plead his cause
and deliver thy soul in safety

8/3/11

118. **in that day**

there shall be a fountain opened,
in that day, in that day
where sin is washed and idols broken,
in that day, in that day.
he shall gather all the nations
in that day, in that day
his feet shall stand upon the mountain
in that day, in that day.

and it shall be one day
known unto the Lord
at evening time it shall be light
one king over all the earth
and they shall say
holiness unto the Lord

there shall be living waters flowing
in that day, in that day
all nations shall come to worship him
in that day, in that day.

and in that day
we shall call upon his name
and he shall call us his people
refined as gold in the flame

9/3/01

119. **Christ's prayer** *(John 17)*

the hour is come glorify your son
that your son may glorify thee
for I have glorified you in the earth
and finished the work you gave me

I pray for them and not the world
for they are not of this world
sanctify them through your truth
For I have given them your word

that they may behold your glory
and the love by which you loved me
that they may be one as we are one
I in them and you in me

6/13/04

120. **prayer of Manasseh**

Almighty Lord God of our fathers
heaven and earth you have made
You fettered the sea and shut up the deep
and sealed it with your glorious name

I have sinned Lord I have sinned
I have no relief and provoked you to anger
forgive me O Lord forgive me
and do not be angry with me forever

I am unworthy to look up to heaven
I am weighed down under my sins
now therefore I bend the knee of my heart
and beg for mercy in all my transgressions

I will praise you as long as I live
You are the God of those who repent
all the host of heaven sing praises

121. Psalm 151

my hand made an instrument
my fingers tuned the strings
who will declare it to my Lord?
the Lord himself is listening.

He himself sent his messenger
He took me from my father's sheep
the youngest and the smallest child
and anointed me with anointing oil.

I went out to meet the enemy
and he called curses down on me
but I pulled out his own sword
and with it I removed his head.

122. always pretend to be crazy around a hostile king

when David realized
that he had been recognized,
he panicked, fearing the worst
from Achish, king of Gath
so right there,
while they were looking at him,
he pretended to go insane
pounding his head on the city gate
and foaming at the mouth,
spit dripping from his beard.
Achish took one look at him
and said to his servants,

"can't you see he's crazy?
why did you let him in here?
don't you think
I have enough
crazy people
to put up with here as it is
without adding another?
GET HIM OUT OF HERE!"

1 Samuel 21

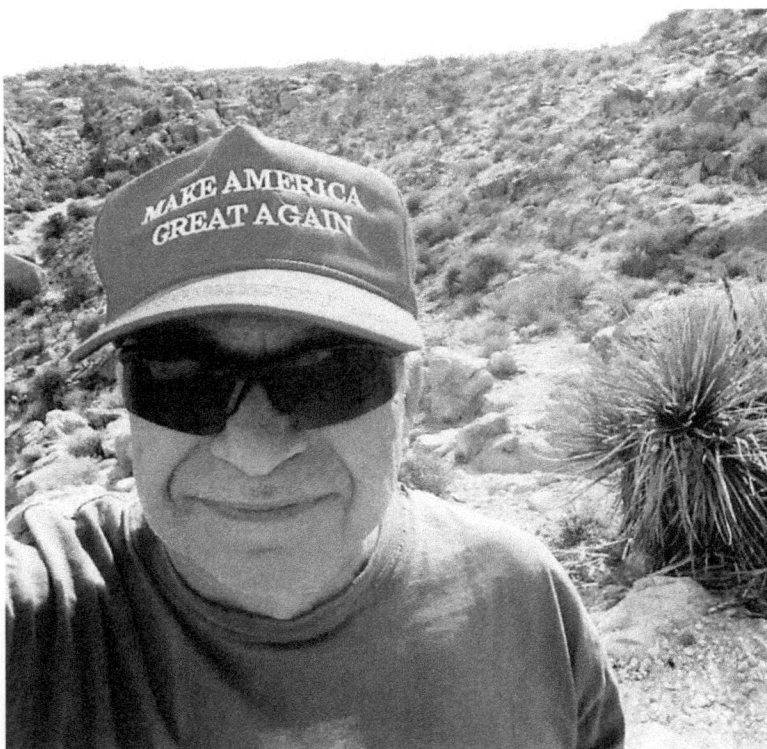

Biography: Eddy Duhan was born in the Long Lake district of Sudbury Ontario, Canada in 1954. His dad died when he was 2 years old and his family moved to North Battleford, Saskatchewan. At 15 he left home with his childhood friend, and blues harmonica legend, Sherman Tank Doucette. They hitchhiked to Vancouver in 1969 together. Within a few months of arriving in Vancouver Eddy became a Christian, and moved into the House of Daniel where he began writing music and poetry. Around 1980, he moved to Orange County, California to become involved in the contemporary Christian music scene, (Eddy got married in 2001 to his wife Jan, and they had a daughter in 2002 named Sarah.) As a Canadian who had overstated his visa' and worked for around 8 years in the underground economy. He eventually obtained amnesty from Ronald Reagan in 1988, then obtained a green card and citizenship. Eddy worked a operator and a telephone repair tech for GTE, Verizon, and Frontier for almost 30 years. He also worked with friend, and record producer, John Andrew Schreiner on numerous worship music projects, the latest being the Union Project, and also the rewriting of music scores for Showtime. He also published 4 poetry books, America (classified) being Eddy's 5th book based on the 2016 election of Hillary R. Clinton and Donald J. Trump.

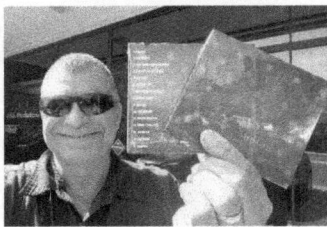

www.ingramcontent.com/pod-product-compliance
Lightning Source LLC
Chambersburg PA
CBHW051827040426

42447CB00006B/401